ROMEO
JULIET
JACK
TUMULT

For Rachel, Adam, Luke, Aaron and Silky

First published 1985 by
Walker Books Ltd,
184-192 Drummond Street,
London NW1 3HP

First printed 1985
Printed and bound by
L.E.G.O., Vicenza, Italy

British Library Cataloguing in Publication Data

Lloyd, David, *1945*
Tumult the rabbit.– (Great escapes)
I. Title II. Firth, Barbara III. Series
823'.914[J] PZ7

ISBN 0-7445-0173-3

TUMULT

THE RABBIT

Written by DAVID LLOYD
Illustrated by BARBARA FIRTH

WALKER BOOKS
LONDON

Every day was a nice day for Tumult, until he first met Rosie Gilfillan.

Nothing ever mattered, until he came out of a borrowed burrow that morning, and began going lippity-lop as easy as can be across a lovely summer meadow.

In a corner of the meadow Rosie Gilfillan was arguing with her boyfriend Horace. 'Of course I like cabbage,' she was saying. 'It's just a stupid present to bring me, that's all.'

'It's a champion cabbage,' Horace said.

'You're a champion cabbage,' Rosie said.

'Bless me!' said Horace, looking over Rosie's shoulder. 'Look at that rabbit!'

Rosie looked, Rosie saw, Rosie wanted.

'Look at its funny ears,' she said, already imagining Tumult in a pie.

Everything about Tumult said 'Take it easy, chuck! Let your ears hang down!'

He was never in a hurry.

He sauntered, he lolloped, he loped.

There was always time to sit up and twitch the nose and whisker the whiskers.

He came to a hedge and went under it.

He lolloped to the pond in the next meadow, and dipped his nose and drank.

He never saw Rosie coming after him with rabbit pie in mind. He never saw her slipping through the hedge, as cunning as a fox in her country ways.

He never saw Horace trudging after her, carrying the cabbage like a baby.

Tumult wandered up the hill, with Rosie coming after him. Rosie was getting very close.

There was a loud bellow in the hedge.

It was Horace with the cabbage.

Horace was badly caught in brambles.

'Rosie!' he bellowed. 'I'm stuck!'

Tumult thumped and jumped and raced lippity-split away.

Rosie went face down in the grass.

'Oh, Horace!' she said, as if everything were always his fault.

The second time Tumult and Rosie met was in the old woods, up on the hill.

Tumult was lying by a fallen elm, just lazing around and dreaming.

Everything about him said 'Take it easy, chuck! Let your ears hang down!'

Rosie was in the woods looking for rabbits to put in pies.

She saw Tumult, but he never saw her.

Rosie was always so cunning.

'Ah, you again,' she thought with pleasure. 'You with the funny ears!'

Rosie came creeping closer and closer.

Cloud shadows moved across the clearing towards the fallen elm, and Rosie moved with them.

Tumult lazed on, lost in his happy-go-lucky dreams.

Now Rosie was so close she could almost touch him.

Rabbit pie was just one step away.

'Rosie!' someone bellowed.

Tumult jumped and thumped and raced lippity-split away.

Rosie went down on her knees at the fallen elm like someone praying.

'Rosie!' someone shouted, coming through the trees. 'I've brought you my champion marrow for a present.'

It was Horace.

Horace loved Rosie.

'Champion marrow!' Rosie said, as if she were calling Horace names.

The third time Tumult met Rosie was in the warren by the stream.

Tumult was having a go at digging a burrow, just to pass the time.

His burrow was not very good, but this didn't matter, because Tumult always borrowed burrows anyway, when he wanted to go underground.

Rosie came into the warren.

'Ah,' she thought, spotting Tumult, 'third time lucky maybe!'

Rosie crept closer.

Tumult scraped away at his burrow, which hardly looked like anything.

Rosie crept closer and closer.

Tumult rested for a moment.

Everything about him said 'Take it easy, chuck! Let your ears hang down!'

Rosie held her breath.

No one made a sound.

Rosie's hands went out like little rockets and caught Tumult round the middle.

Tumult couldn't go lippity-split.
He couldn't go lippity-lop.
He couldn't go lippity-anything.
He was well and truly caught.

Rosie came out of the warren holding him very tight.

She was smiling.

Horace stepped out from a hiding place beside the path and bellowed.

'Stop, Rosie, stop!'

But it was too late.
Rosie trod on a mat of ferns and
the ground gave way beneath her.
She fell into a pit with Tumult.
There were vegetables on the floor.
Horace peered over the edge of the pit.

'Rosie,' he said.
Horace loved Rosie.
'I dug the pit to catch the rabbit,'
he said. 'The vegetables were bait.'
'Oh, Horace,' Rosie said out of the pit.
'It was going to be a present,' Horace said.

Now Horace had to rescue Rosie.

But first Rosie had to pass him Tumult.

Horace held Tumult gently for a moment, looking at his funny, hang-down ears.

Then he put him on the ground to have both hands free for Rosie.

'Horace!' Rosie cried out.

Tumult thumped and jumped and raced lippity-split away.

He was in a most amazing hurry.

Everything about him said 'Go, chuck, go! Button your ears and beat it!'

There are seven animals in the gang today. They have all had great escapes. They live together and travel together. They are friends.

Today they are all in a cave by the sea, and it is Tumult's turn to tell the story.

'Every day was always a nice day,' he begins, 'until I first met Rosie Gilfillan.'

And the story which he tells is the story you just heard.

WALDO
LADY LOUDLY
MOT